HSP Math

UNIT 5

Harcourt

SCHOOL PUBLISHERS

Visit *The Learning Site!*
www.harcourtschool.com

Harcourt

SCHOOL PUBLISHERS

THE WORLD ALMANAC FOR KIDS

HSP Math

Part Number 9997-85170-6

9 10 11 12   0914   15 14 13 12

4500386266

Senior Authors

Evan M. Maletsky
Professor Emeritus
Montclair State University
Upper Montclair, New Jersey

Joyce McLeod
Visiting Professor, Retired
Rollins College
Winter Park, Florida

Authors

Karen S. Norwood
Associate Professor of
    Mathematics Education
North Carolina State University
Raleigh, North Carolina

Tom Roby
Associate Professor
    of Mathematics
Director, Quantitative
    Learning Center
University of Connecticut
Storrs, Connecticut

James A. Mendoza Epperson
Associate Professor
Department of Mathematics
The University of Texas
    at Arlington
Arlington, Texas

Juli K. Dixon
Associate Professor of
    Mathematics Education
University of Central Florida
Orlando, Florida

Janet K. Scheer
Executive Director
Create-A-Vision
Foster City, California

David G. Wright
Professor
Department of Mathematics
Brigham Young University
Provo, Utah

David D. Molina
Program Director, Retired
The Charles A. Dana Center
The University of Texas
    at Austin

Jennie M. Bennett
Mathematics Teacher
Houston Independent
    School District
Houston, Texas

Lynda Luckie
Director, K–12 Mathematics
Gwinnett County Public Schools
Suwanee, Georgia

Angela G. Andrews
Assistant Professor of
    Math Education
National Louis University
Lisle, Illinois

Vicki Newman
Classroom Teacher
McGaugh Elementary School
Los Alamitos Unified
    School District
Seal Beach, California

Barbara Montalto
Mathematics Consultant
Assistant Director of
    Mathematics, Retired
Texas Education Agency
Austin, Texas

Minerva Cordero-Epperson
Associate Professor of Mathematics
    and Associate Dean of the
    Honors College
The University of Texas
    at Arlington
Arlington, Texas

Program Consultants and Specialists

Russell Gersten
Director, Instructional
    Research Group
Long Beach, California
Professor Emeritus of
    Special Education
University of Oregon
Eugene, Oregon

Michael DiSpezio
Writer and On-Air Host,
    JASON Project
North Falmouth,
    Massachusetts

Concepcion Molina
Southwest Educational
    Development Lab
Austin, Texas

Rebecca Valbuena
Language Development
    Specialist
Stanton Elementary School
Glendora, California

Valerie Johse
Elementary Math Specialist
Office of Curriculum
    & Instruction
Pearland I.S.D.
Pearland, Texas

Robin C. Scarcella
Professor and Director,
    Program of Academic
    English and ESL
University of California, Irvine
Irvine, California

Lydia Song
Mathematics Program
    Specialist
Costa Mesa, California

Tyrone Howard
Assistant Professor,
    UCLA Graduate School
    of Education—
    Information Studies
University of California
    at Los Angeles
Los Angeles, California

Anne M. Goodrow
Associate Professor,
    Elementary Education
Rhode Island College
Providence, Rhode Island

Unit 5

Helping Hands

written by Ann Lee

In this story you will also TALK Math and WRITE Math.

Family note: This story will help your child identify objects by size.

A

Today I help Dad in the garden.

We wear our gloves.

Circle the bigger glove.

Science

What plants do you see?

Dad puts on his sun hat.

I put on mine.

Circle the smaller hat.

Science

How are most plants the same?

c

Dad fills his watering can.

I fill one, too.

Circle the watering can that holds more.

Science

What do plants need?

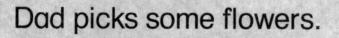

Dad picks some flowers.

I pick some, too.

Circle the smallest flower.

Science

What are some plants that have flowers?

E

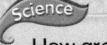

We surprised Mom!

Circle who has the biggest smile.

Science

How are all flowers alike?

F

Name _____

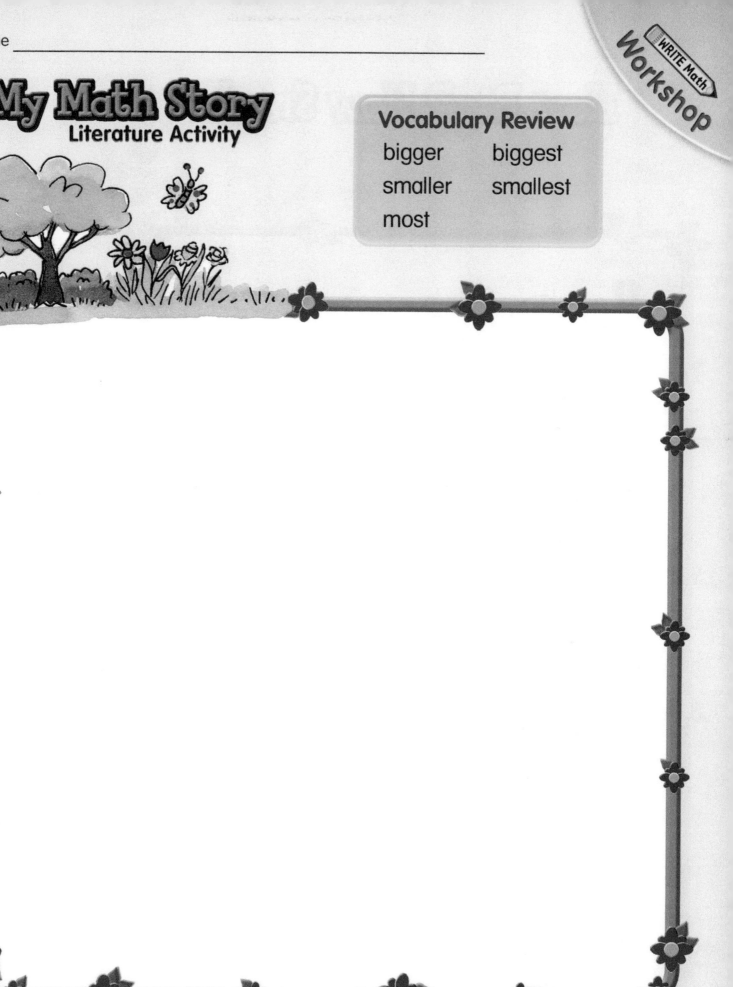

My Math Story
Literature Activity

Vocabulary Review

bigger   biggest

smaller   smallest

most

DIRECTIONS Draw a story about plants.
Tell which plants are smaller and which plants are bigger.

G

How Big? How Small?

1.

2.

3.

DIRECTIONS Look at the pictures. **I.** Draw a
butterfly that is smaller. **2.** Draw a watering can
that is bigger. **3.** Draw a flower that is the same size.

H

© Harcourt

UNIT 5

School Home CONNECTION

Dear Family,

My class started Unit 5 today. I will learn how to measure objects. I will also learn about calendar, time, and temperature. Here are some vocabulary words and activities for us to share.

Love, _____

Vocabulary Power

Key Math Vocabulary

Measure to find size, weight, capacity, length, height, etc.

Clock an instrument that tells time

Vocabulary Activity

Math on the Move

Show your child 3 objects of different lengths and ask him or her to place them in order starting with the shortest.

GO ONLINE

Technology
Multimedia Math Gloassary link at
www.harcourtschool.com/hspmath

School Home CONNECTION

Remember This Your child may already know how to compare the length of two objects by holding them together.

Calendar Activity

January

Sunday	Monday	Tuesday	Wednesday	Thursday	Friday	Saturday
				1	2	3
4	5	6	7	8	9	10
11	12	13	14	15	16	17
18	19	20	21	22	23	24
25	26	27	28	29	30	31

Ask your child if there are more Mondays or more Fridays in this month.

Practice (after pages 263 and 264)

Have your child circle a day on the calendar. Then have him or her tell you what day it will be tomorrow and what day it was yesterday.

Practice (after pages 267 and 268)

Have your child circle the first day of the month and then mark an x on the last day of the month.

Literature

Look for these books in a library. Ask your child to point out math vocabulary words as you read each book together.

The Best Bug Parade.
Murphy, Stuart J.
HarperCollins, 1996.

Mighty Maddie.
Murphy, Stuart J.
HarperCollins, 2004.

Daddy Goes to Work.
Asim, Jabari.
Little, Brown and Company, 2006.

Measurement
Theme: How Does Your Garden Grow?

Name _____

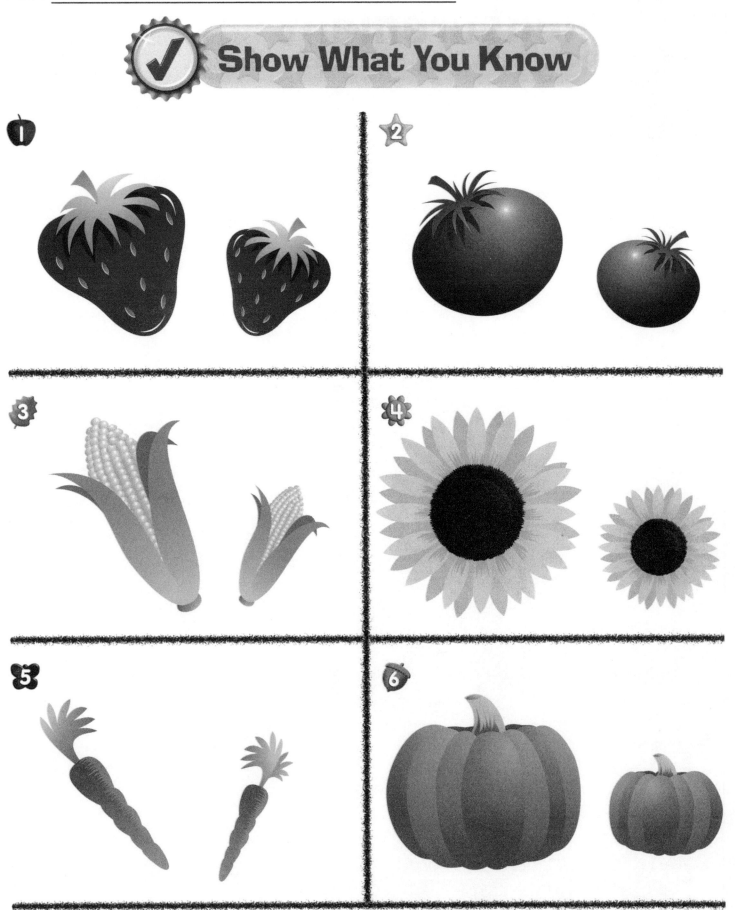

✓ Show What You Know

1

2

3

4

5

6

DIRECTIONS 1–3. Circle the object that is bigger. 4–6. Circle the object that is smaller.

🏠 **Family Note:** This page checks your child's understanding of important concepts and skills needed for success in Chapter 9.

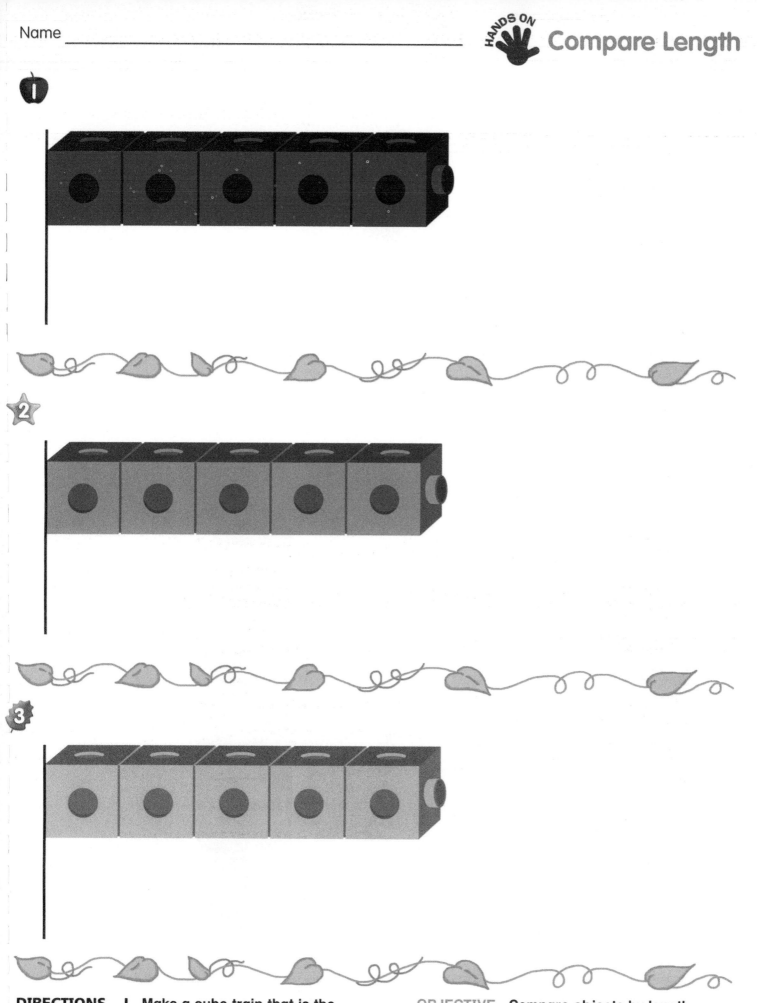

Compare Length

1

2

3

DIRECTIONS 1. Make a cube train that is the same length. Draw the cube train.
2. Make a cube train that is shorter. Draw the cube train. 3. Make a cube train that is longer. Draw the cube train.

OBJECTIVE • Compare objects by length.

Chapter 9 • Lesson 1

two hundred thirty-three **233**

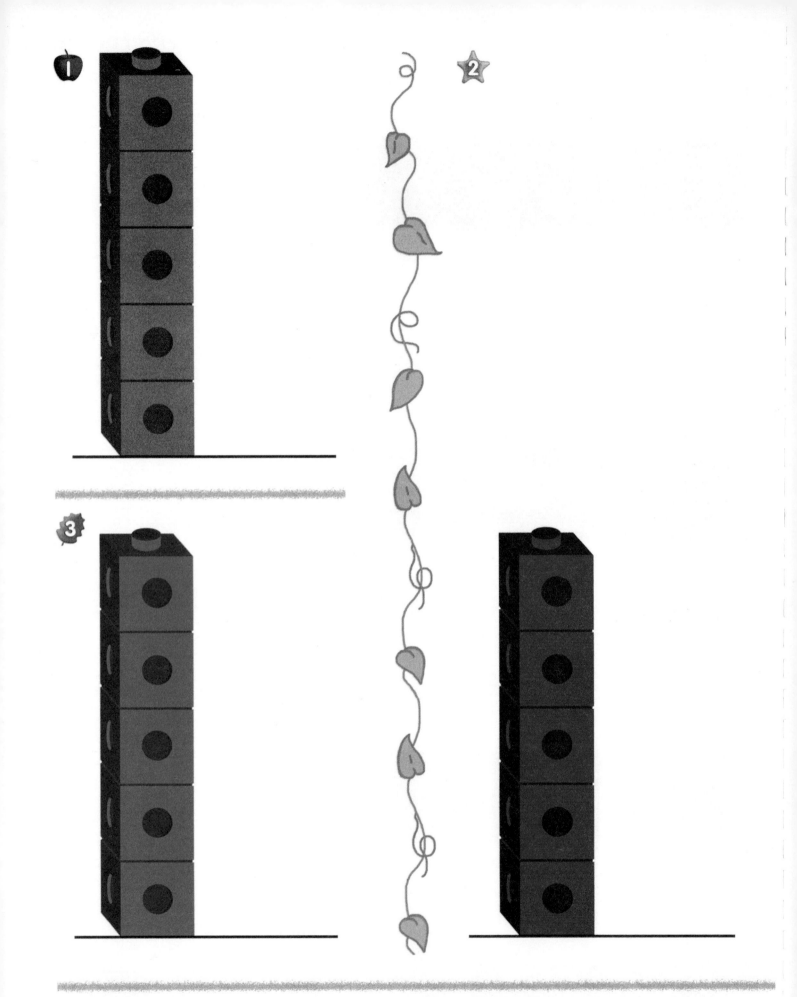

DIRECTIONS **I.** Make a cube train that is shorter. Draw the cube train. **2.** Make a cube train that is taller. Draw the cube train. **3.** Make a cube train that is the same height. Draw the cube train.

 HOME ACTIVITY • Show your child a pencil, and ask him or her to find an object that is longer than the pencil. Repeat with an object that is shorter than the pencil.

234 two hundred thirty-four

DIRECTIONS Find a classroom object that is shorter than the crayon and an object that is longer than the crayon. Draw the objects in order from shortest to longest.

OBJECTIVE • Order objects by length.

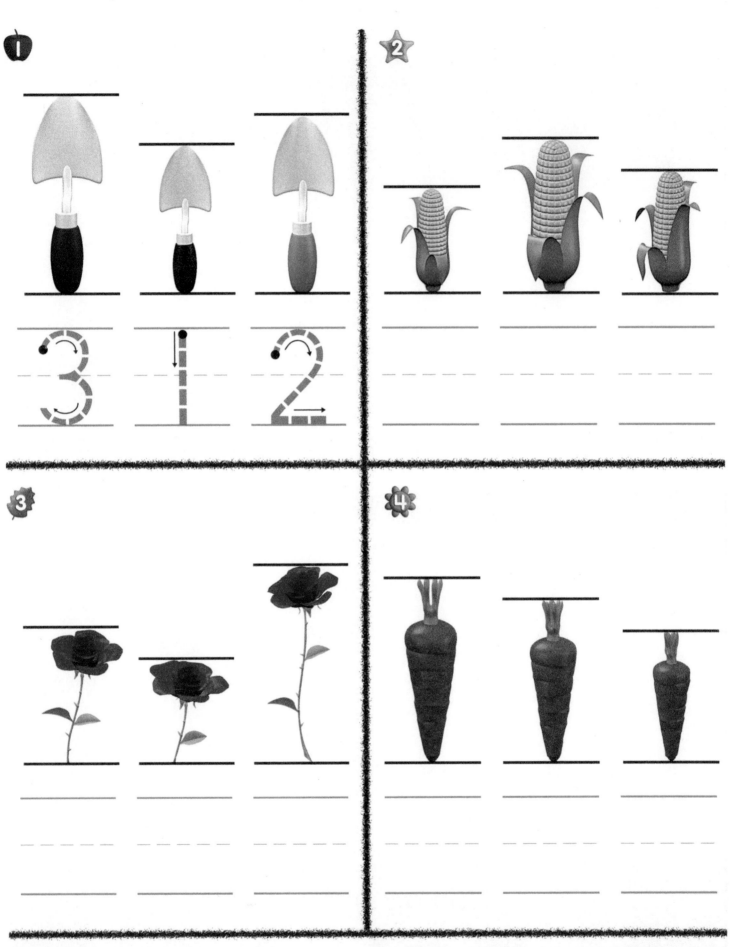

3 1 2

DIRECTIONS 1–4. Write the numbers *1, 2,* and *3* to order the objects from shortest to longest.

 HOME ACTIVITY • Give your child three shoes of different lengths. Have him or her trace around each shoe on paper and write *1, 2,* and *3* in the shoe shapes to order them from shortest to longest.

© Harcourt

Name _____

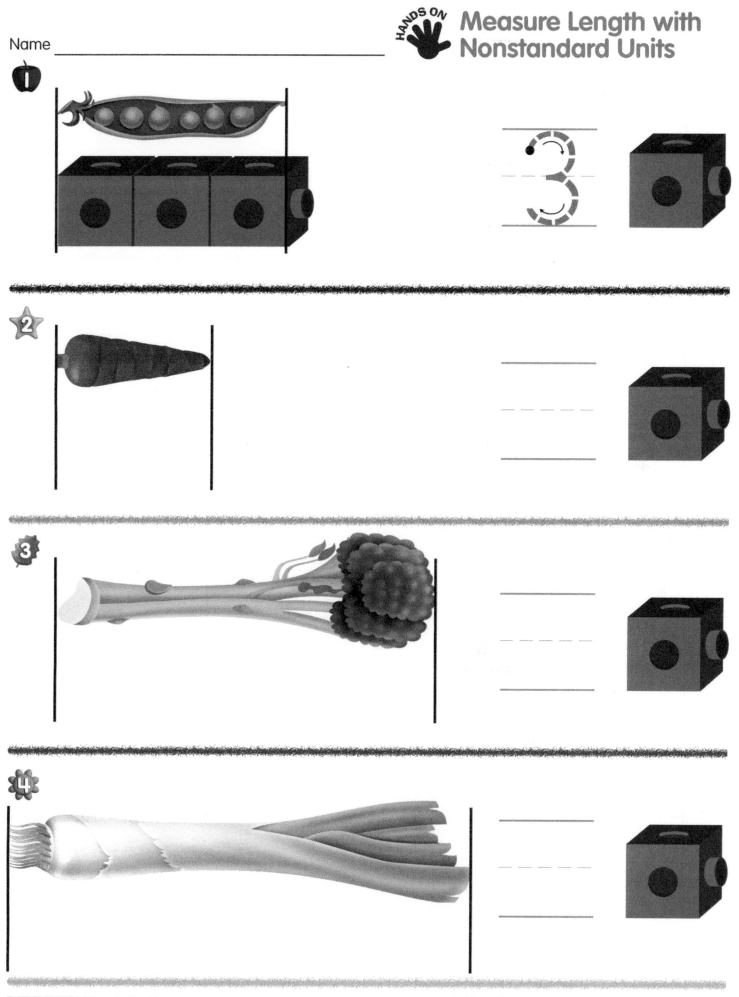

1

3

2

3

4

DIRECTIONS 1–4. Use cubes to measure the vegetable. Write about how many cubes long it is.

OBJECTIVE • Measure length with nonstandard units.

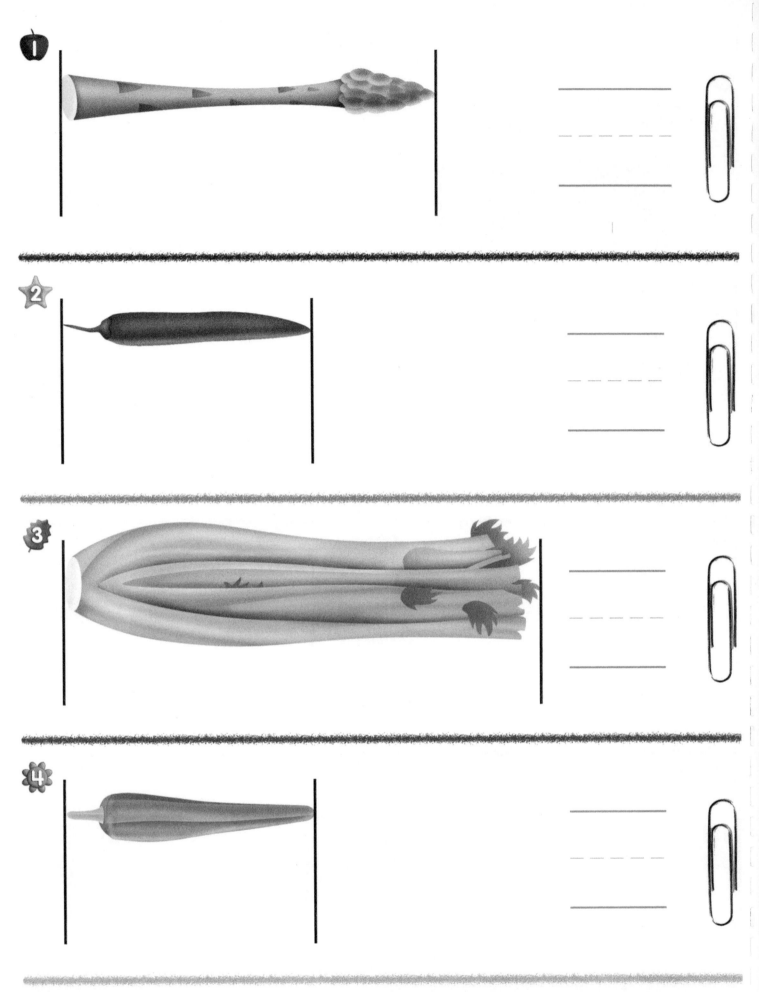

DIRECTIONS 1–4. Use paper clips to measure the vegetable. Write about how many paper clips long it is.

HOME ACTIVITY · Give your child a raw vegetable like a stalk of celery or a carrot. Help him or her trace around the outline on paper and use paper clips to measure its length.

Name _____

Estimate	Classroom Object	Measure

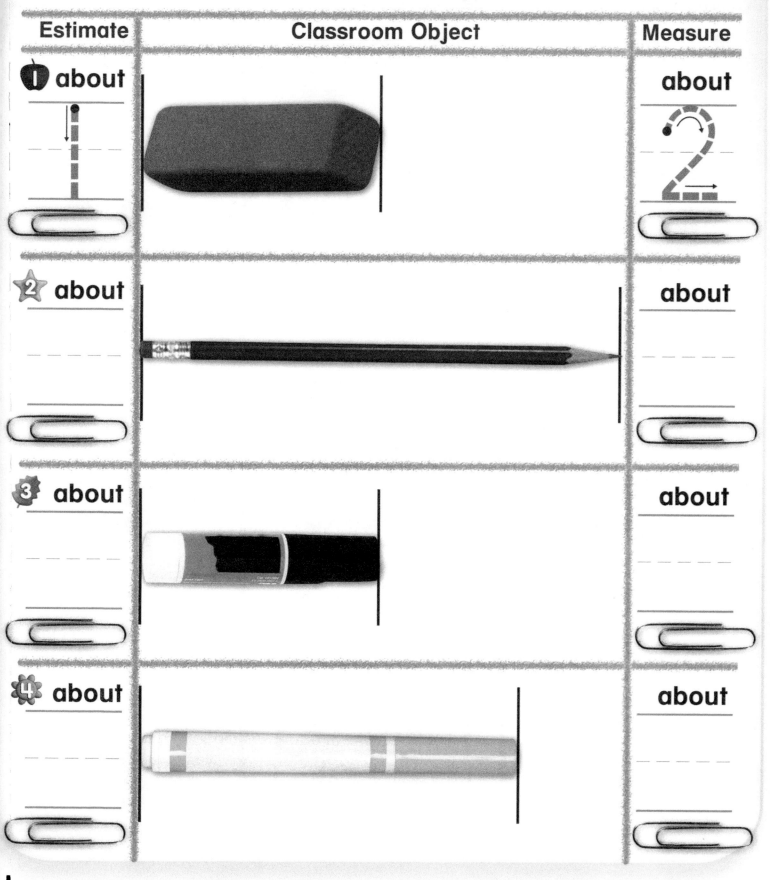

1 about _____

about _____

2 about _____

about _____

3 about _____

about _____

4 about _____

about _____

DIRECTIONS 1–4. Find the object in the classroom. Estimate about how many paper clips long it is. Write your estimate. Use paper clips to measure the object. Write about how many paper clips long it is.

OBJECTIVE • Solve problems by using the strategy *estimate and measure.*

Chapter 9 • Lesson 4

two hundred thirty-nine **239**

Estimate	Classroom Object	Measure

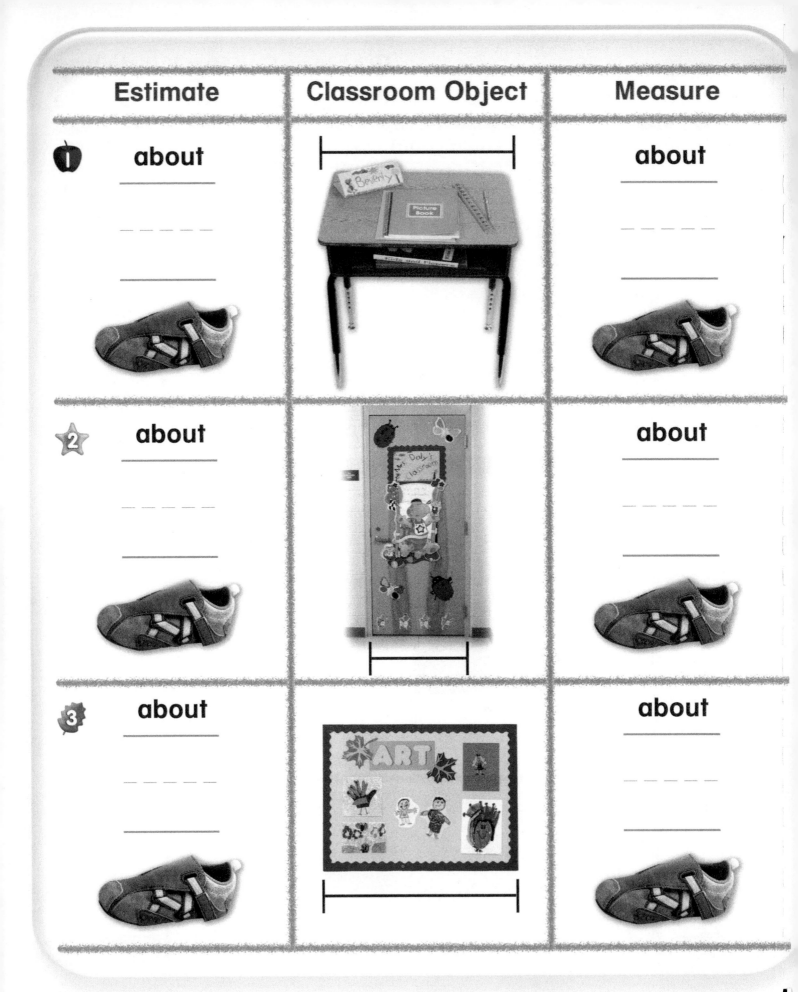

1 about   about

2 about   about

3 about   about

DIRECTIONS 1–3. Estimate about how many shoes long the object is, and write your estimate. Measure the object and write the measurement.

 HOME ACTIVITY · Ask your child to estimate and then measure about how many hand lengths long the kitchen table is.

Name _____

✓ Mid Chapter 9 Review

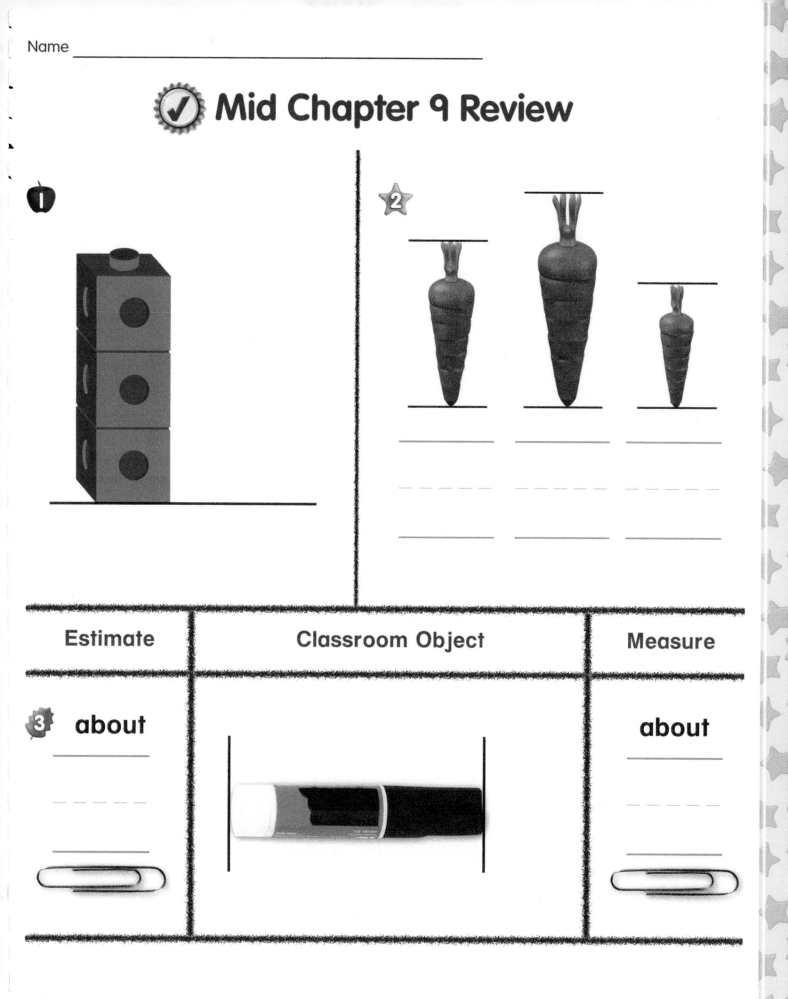

Estimate	Classroom Object	Measure
3 **about** _____		**about** _____

DIRECTIONS 1. Make a cube train that is shorter. Draw the cube train. 2. Write the numbers *1*, *2*, and *3* to order the objects from shortest to longest. 3. Find the object in the classroom. Estimate about how many paper clips long it is. Write your estimate. Use paper clips to measure the object. Write about how many paper clips long it is.

Chapter 9   two hundred forty-one **241**

Name _____

✓ Cumulative Review

1

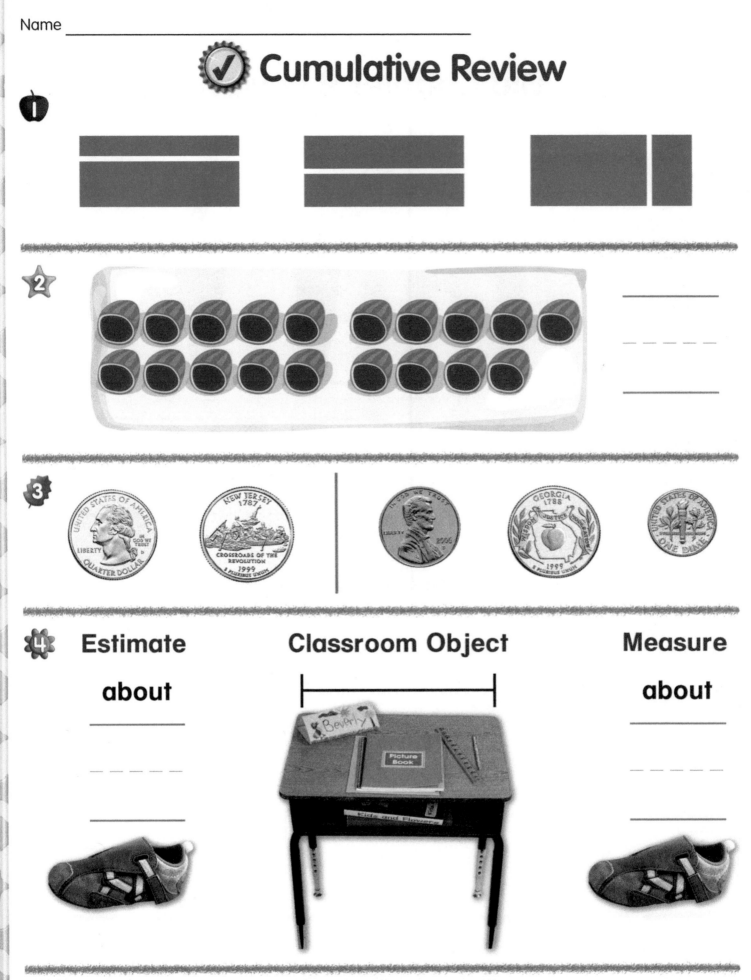

2

_____
_ _ _ _ _ _ _ _
_____

3

4 Estimate   Classroom Object   Measure

about   about

_____   _____
_ _ _ _ _ _ _ _   _ _ _ _ _ _ _ _
_____   _____

DIRECTIONS **I.** Circle the figure with a line that makes two matching parts. **2.** How many pieces of fruit? Write the number. **3.** Name the coin on the left. Circle the coin with the same value on the right. **4.** Estimate about how many shoes long the object is and write your estimate. Measure the object and write the measurement.

Name _____

HANDS ON Explore Capacity

about

handfuls

	about _____ - - - - - - _____ **handfuls**
	about _____ - - - - - - _____ **handfuls**
	about _____ - - - - - - _____ **handfuls**

DIRECTIONS Use drinking cups like the cups pictured. Fill each cup with handfuls of rice. Write about how many handfuls each cup holds.

OBJECTIVE • Explore capacity.

Chapter 9 • Lesson 5

two hundred forty-three **243**

about 4

about

about

about

DIRECTIONS Use drinking cups like the cups pictured. Fill each cup with scoops of rice. Write about how many scoops each cup holds.

 HOME ACTIVITY · Show your child two different-sized cups. Have your child use a small scoop to tell you how many scoops are in each cup.

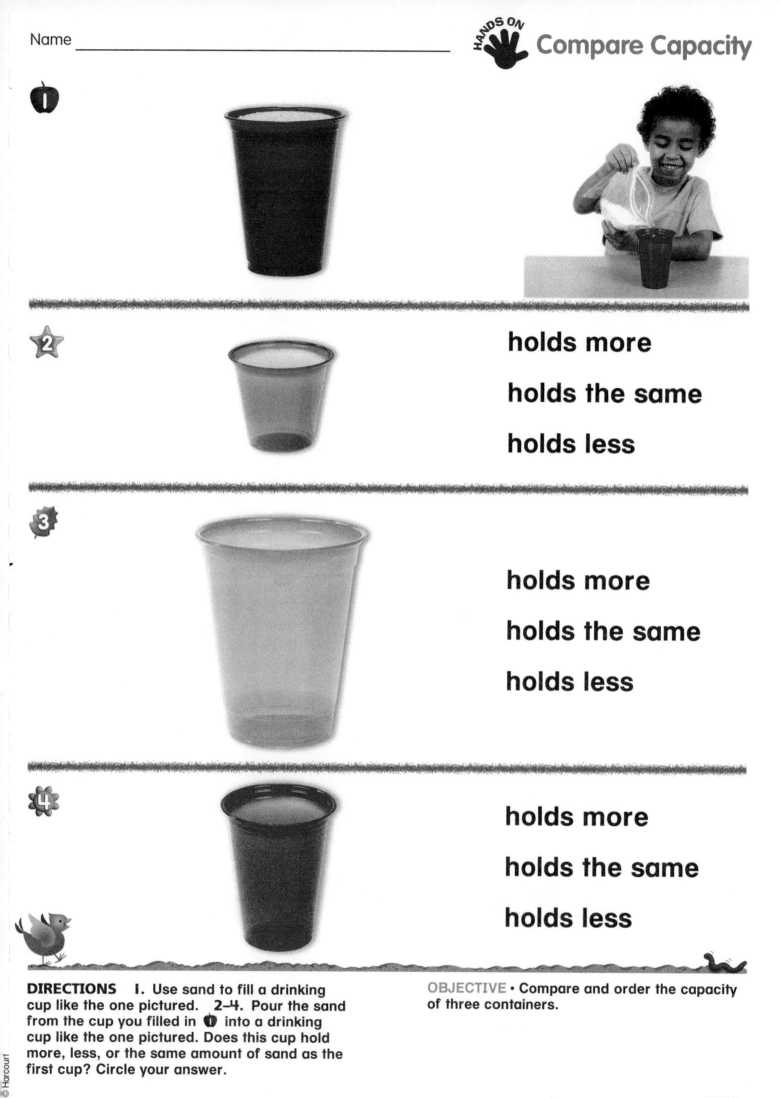

HANDS ON Compare Capacity

①

② holds more

holds the same

holds less

③ holds more

holds the same

holds less

④ holds more

holds the same

holds less

DIRECTIONS **I.** Use sand to fill a drinking cup like the one pictured. **2–4.** Pour the sand from the cup you filled in **①** into a drinking cup like the one pictured. Does this cup hold more, less, or the same amount of sand as the first cup? Circle your answer.

OBJECTIVE • Compare and order the capacity of three containers.

Chapter 9 • Lesson 6

two hundred forty-five **245**

© Harcourt

DIRECTIONS Fill three different-sized drinking cups with sand. Use a different color to draw the cups in order, beginning with the cup that holds the least amount of sand.

 HOME ACTIVITY · Show your child a pan. Have him or her find a pan that holds less and a pan that holds more. Then ask your child to place the pans in order from the pan that holds the least to the pan that holds the most.

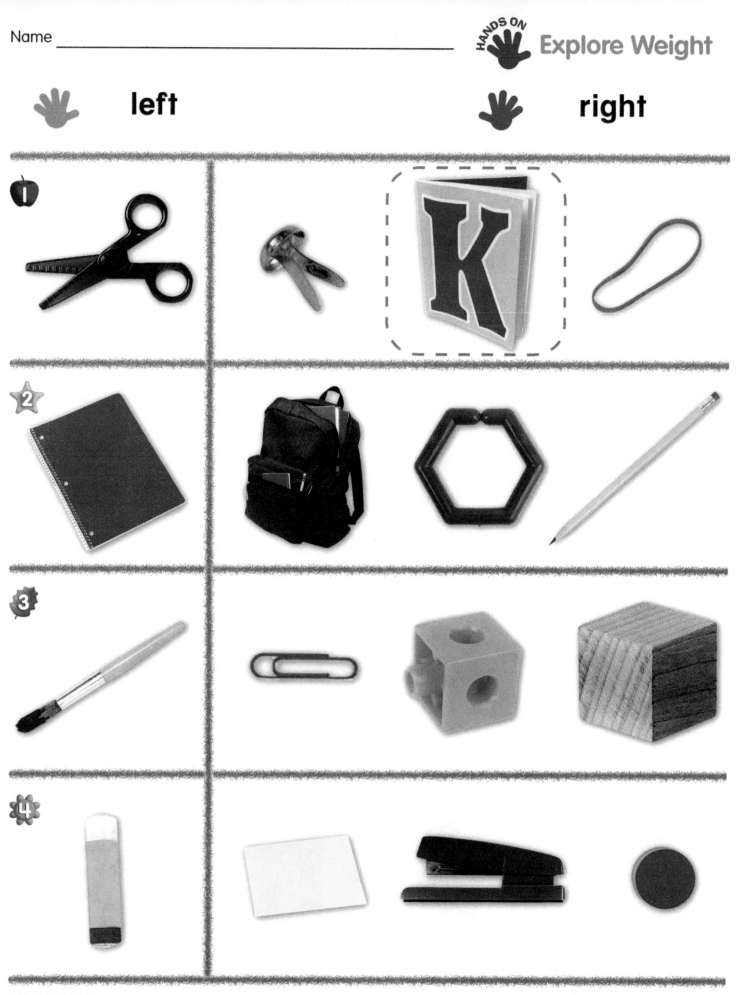

Explore Weight

left   right

DIRECTIONS 1–4. Find the first object in the row, and hold it in your left hand. Find the rest of the objects in the row, and take turns holding each object in your right hand. Circle the object that is heavier than the object in your left hand.

OBJECTIVE • Explore objects by weight.

© Harcourt

left   **right**

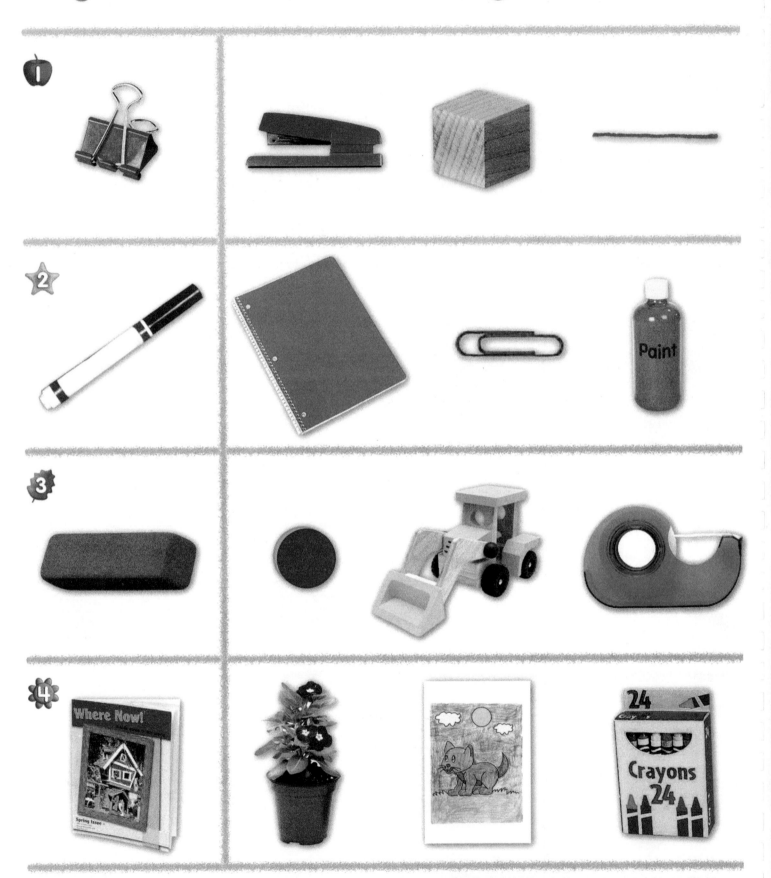

DIRECTIONS 1–4. **Find the first object in the row, and hold it in your left hand. Find the rest of the objects in the row, and take turns holding each object in your right hand. Circle the object that is lighter than the object in your left hand.**

 HOME ACTIVITY • Give your child a small household object. Have him or her find another household object that is lighter.

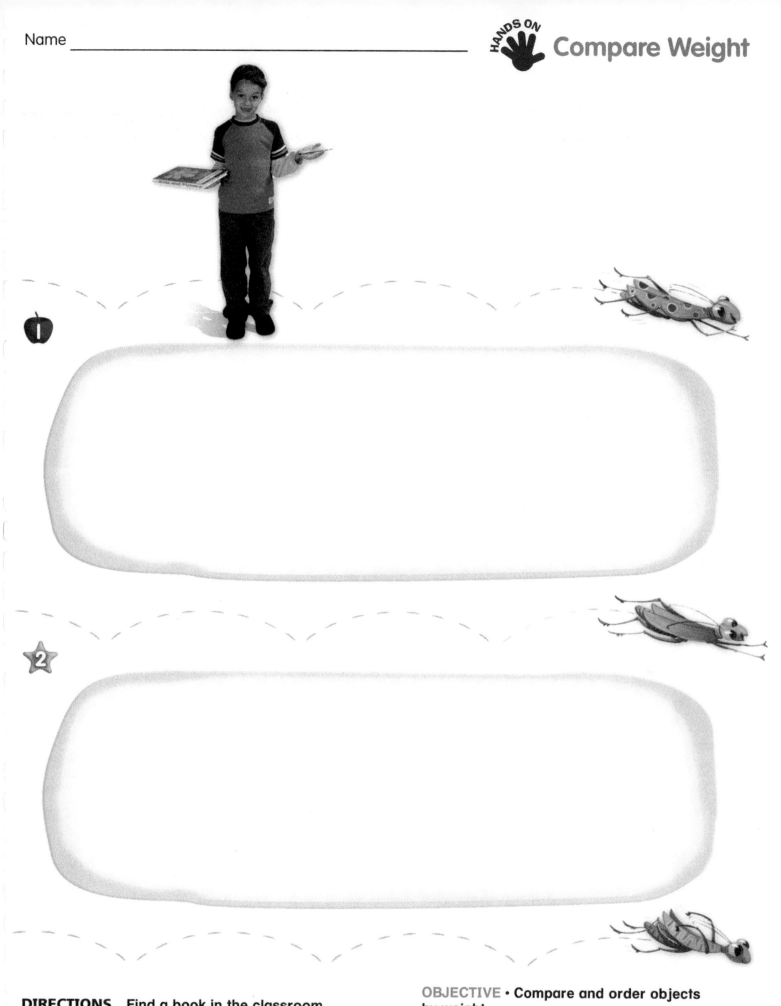

1

2

DIRECTIONS Find a book in the classroom.
1. Find a classroom object that is lighter than the book and draw it in the work space.
2. Find a classroom object that is heavier than the book and draw it in the work space.

OBJECTIVE • Compare and order objects by weight.

DIRECTIONS Find three classroom objects that have different weights. Draw the objects in order from lightest to heaviest.

HOME ACTIVITY · Give your child three objects of clearly different weights. Have him or her place them in order from lightest to heaviest.

Name _____

Explore Area

HANDS ON

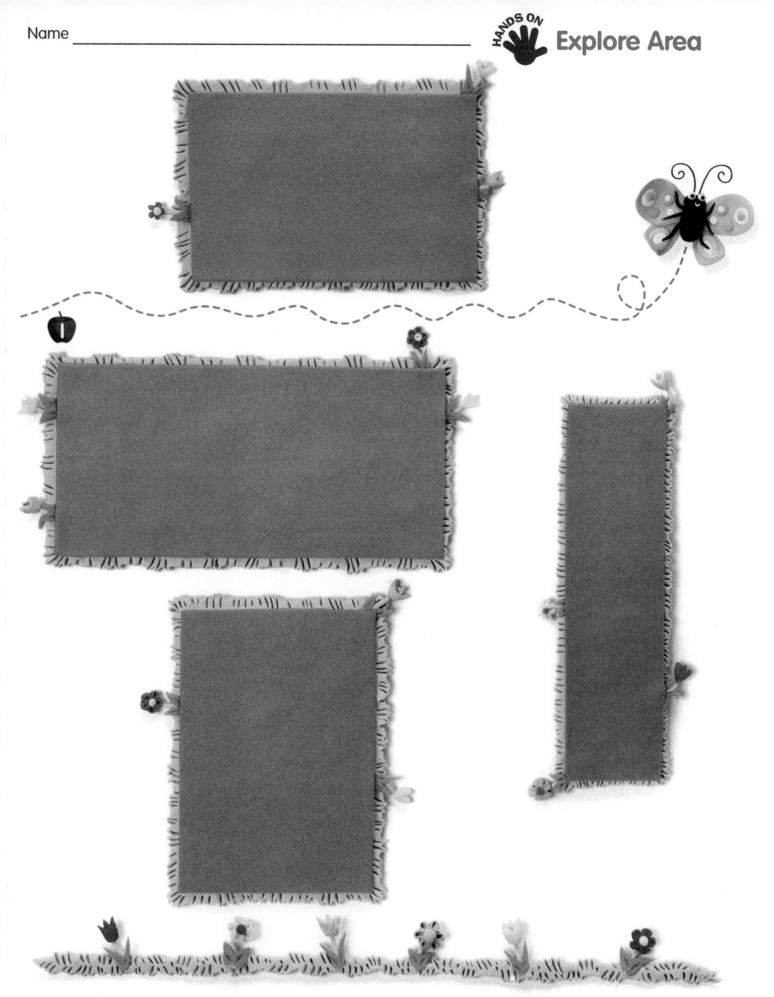

DIRECTIONS 1. Use color tiles to find the garden that has the same area as the model garden at the top of the page. Circle the garden.

OBJECTIVE • Explore the area of a surface.

© Harcourt

Chapter 9 • Lesson 9

two hundred fifty-one **251**

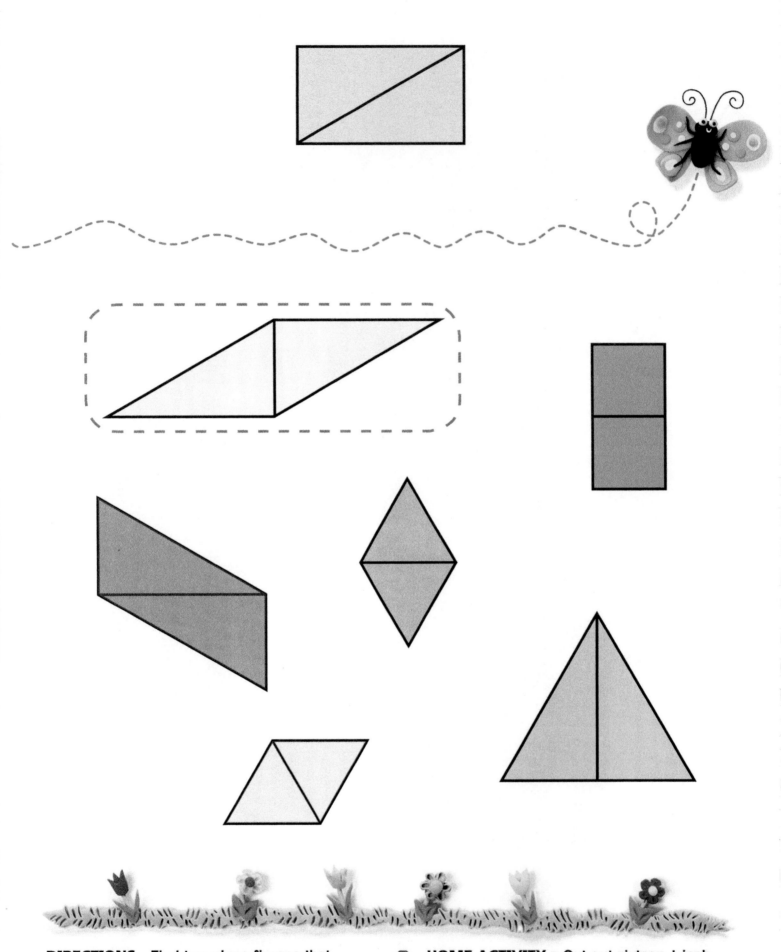

DIRECTIONS Find two plane figures that make the figure at the top of the page. Use these two figures to find the figures that have the same area as the model at the top of the page. Circle these figures.

HOME ACTIVITY • Cut out sixteen 1-inch green squares. Have your child use the figures to make a garden that has four squares on each side. Then have your child use the squares to make a garden.

© Harcourt

Name _____

estimate

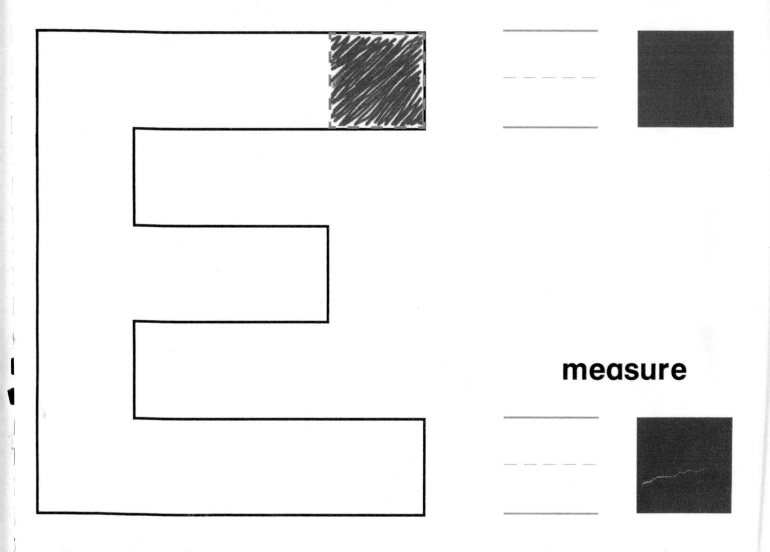

measure

DIRECTIONS Estimate how many color tiles it will take to cover the area of the letter. Write your estimate. Use color tiles to measure the area. Write how many color tiles it takes. Trace and color the tiles.

OBJECTIVE • Solve problems by using the skill *use estimation.*

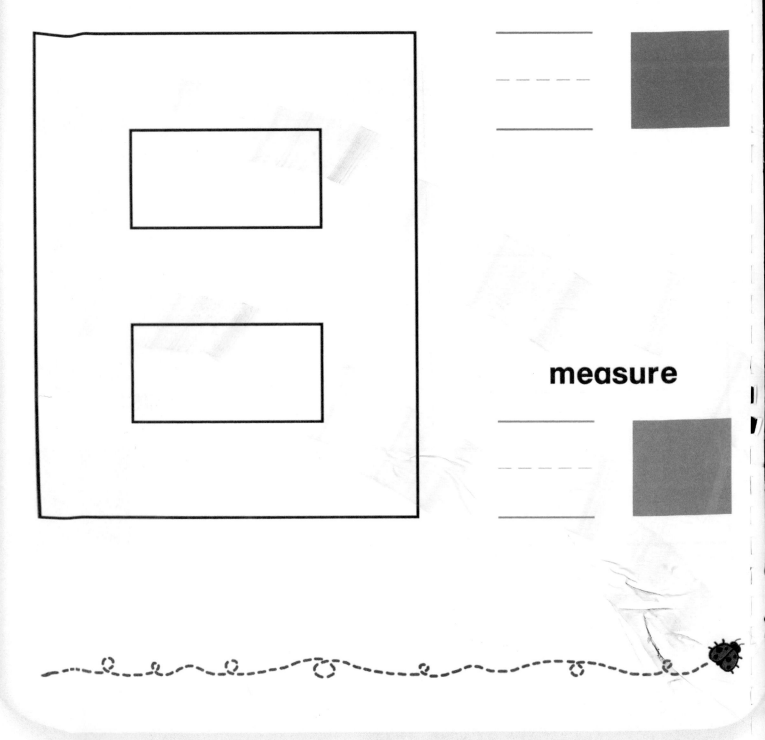

estimate

measure

DIRECTIONS Estimate how many color tiles it will take to cover the area of the number. Write your estimate. Use color tiles to measure the area. Write how many color tiles it takes. Trace and color the tiles.

HOME ACTIVITY · Cut out 1-inch squares. Use these squares to draw a block numeral. Have your child estimate how many squares it will take to cover the area. Then have him or her use the squares to measure and check the estimate.

254 two hundred fifty-four

© Harcourt

Name _____

Connecting Cube Challenge

DIRECTIONS: Take turns with a partner tossing the number cube. Move your marker that number of spaces. If a player lands on a cube he or she takes a cube and makes a cube train. At the end of the game, players compare cube trains. The player with the longer cube train must find a classroom object longer than his or her cube train. The player with the shorter cube train must find a classroom object shorter than his or her cube train. If the cube trains are the same length, players must find a classroom object the same length as the cube trains.

MATERIALS: game markers, number cube (1-6), connecting cubes

Chapter 9

Math Power • Which Holds the Most?

Estimate	Container	Measure
about		about
about		about
about		about

DIRECTIONS Find containers like the ones pictured. Estimate about how many cups of rice will fill each container. Write your estimate. Use cups of rice to fill each container. Write about how many cups were used to fill each container. Circle the container that holds the most rice.

Name _____

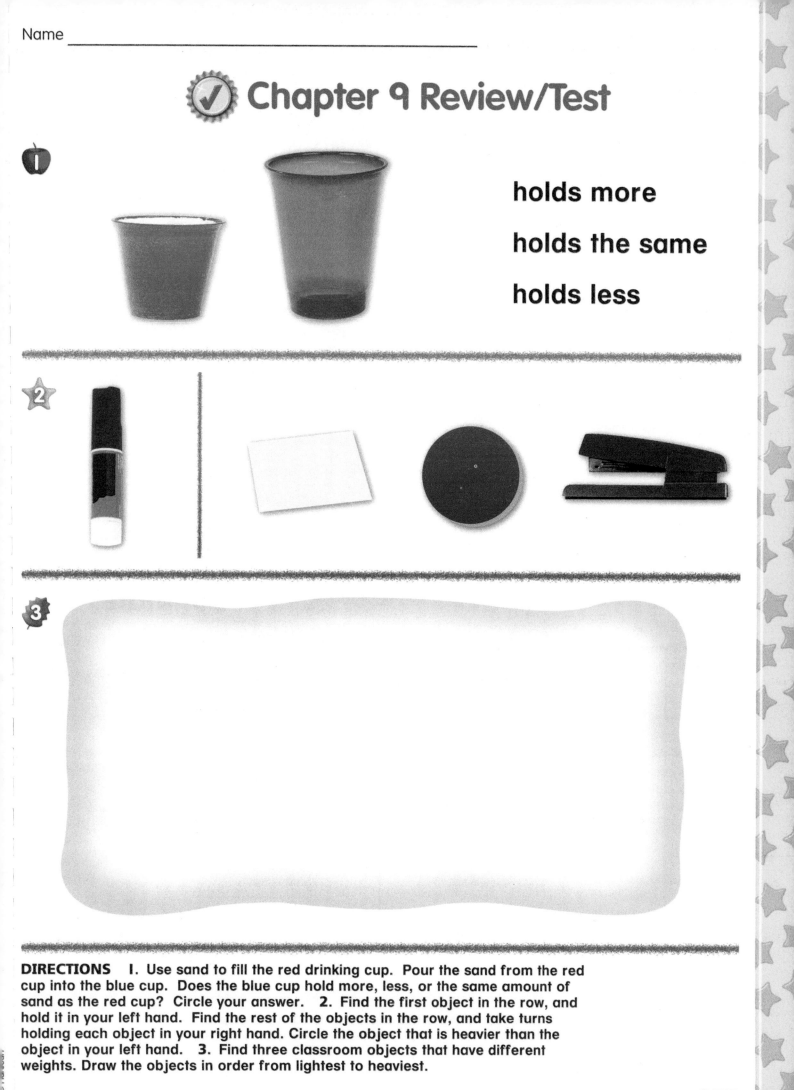

1

holds more

holds the same

holds less

2

3

DIRECTIONS 1. Use sand to fill the red drinking cup. Pour the sand from the red cup into the blue cup. Does the blue cup hold more, less, or the same amount of sand as the red cup? Circle your answer. 2. Find the first object in the row, and hold it in your left hand. Find the rest of the objects in the row, and take turns holding each object in your right hand. Circle the object that is heavier than the object in your left hand. 3. Find three classroom objects that have different weights. Draw the objects in order from lightest to heaviest.

✅ Cumulative Review

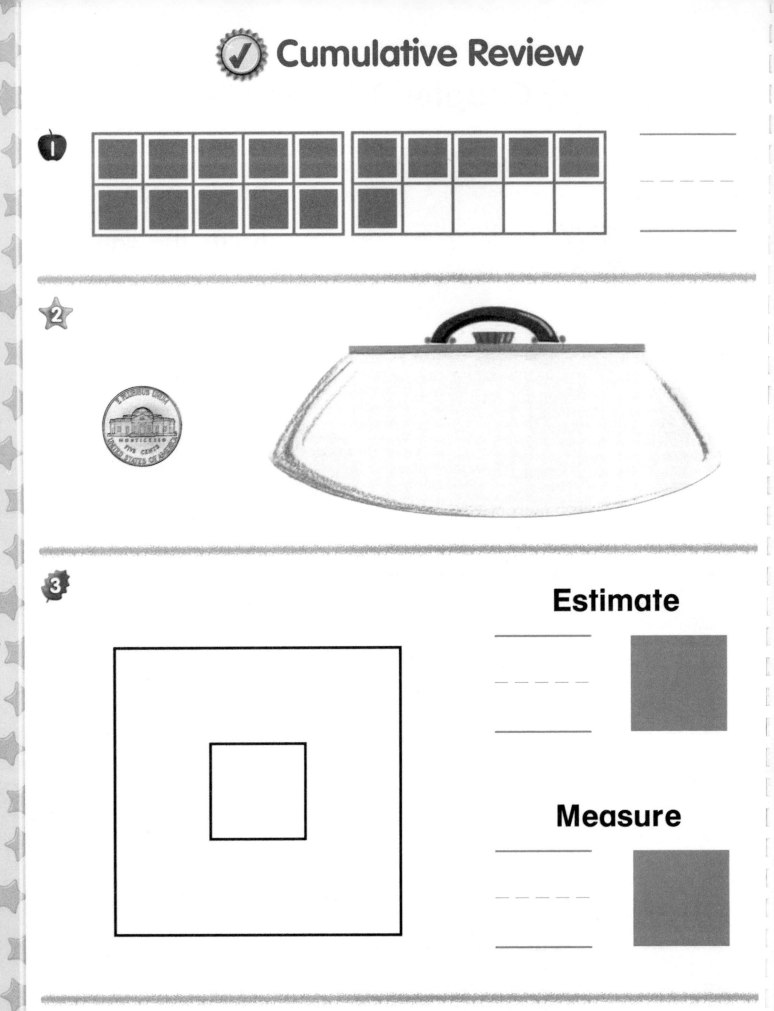

Estimate

Measure

DIRECTIONS 1. How many color tiles? Write the number. 2. Use pennies to show the value of the coin. Draw the pennies. 3. Estimate how many color tiles it will take to cover the area of the number. Write your estimate. Use color tiles to measure the area. Write how many color tiles it takes. Trace and color the tiles.

Explore Calendar, Time, and Temperature

Theme: Day Planner

Name _____

First	**Next**	**Last**
❶		
⭐2		
🍁3		

DIRECTIONS 1. Draw a picture to show what would come first. 2. Draw a picture to show what would come next. 3. Draw a picture to show what would come last.

🏠 **FAMILY NOTE:** This page checks your child's understanding of important concepts and skills needed for success in Chapter 10.

260 two hundred sixty

Name _____

Days of the Week

1

Sunday | Monday | Tuesday | Wednesday | Thursday | Friday | Saturday

2

Tuesday

Friday

Sunday

Wednesday

Saturday

Monday

Thursday

DIRECTIONS 1. Point to and say each day of the week. 2. Number the days in order, beginning with Sunday.

OBJECTIVE • Identify the days of the week.

Chapter 10 • Lesson 1

two hundred sixty-one **261**

June

Sunday	Monday	Tuesday	Wednesday	Thursday	Friday	Saturday
	1	2	3	4	5	6
7	8	9	10	11	12	13
14	15	16	17	18	19	20
21	22	23	24	25	26	27
28	29	30				

2. Wednesdays

4 _____

3. Mondays

_____

_____

4. Fridays

_____

5. Days in June

_____

_____

DIRECTIONS 1. Use red to color all the Sundays. Use blue to color all the Fridays. 2. Write how many Wednesdays are in this month. 3. Write how many Mondays are in this month. 4. Write how many Fridays are in this month. 5. Write how many days are in June.

 HOME ACTIVITY • Show your child a calendar for the current month. Have him or her point to the days of the week as you both say them aloud. Have your child count the number of Wednesdays in the month.

Sunday

Monday

Tuesday

Wednesday

Thursday

Friday

Saturday

yesterday

today

tomorrow

DIRECTIONS Draw a line from *today* to the name of the day. Trace the word. Trace the name of the day before today. Draw a line from that day to *yesterday*. Trace the name of the day after today, and draw a line to *tomorrow*.

OBJECTIVE • **Use the days of the week to describe a sequence of events.**

morning

afternoon

evening

———

- - -

———

morning

afternoon

evening

———

- - -

———

morning

afternoon

evening

———

- - -

———

DIRECTIONS Look at each picture. Circle the time of day that this would probably happen. Use numbers to show the order.

HOME ACTIVITY · Have your child draw three pictures, showing what he or she does in the morning, in the afternoon, and in the evening. Have him or her number the pictures to show the order.